THE REMINDER

Reconnecting With the Forgotten You

Lyvonne Copeland

Cover designed by Robin King

ISBN-13: 978-0692995020

DEDICATION

This book is dedicated to the women who have lost their voice, vision and vitality for life. Your voice matters. The vision matters. So *remind* yourself, that you matter.

CONTENTS

ACKNOWLEDGMENTS

First and foremost, I give thanks to God for choosing me for such a purpose. I am thankful that He trusts me with His word. My heart's desire is to see His desire for my life manifested.

To my husband, Tommy, thank you for pushing me to start writing and supporting me.

This has been a journey and I thank every person who prayed, encouraged and motivated me.

How Did I Get Here?

God why is my spirit troubled? Why is my mind in turmoil? Why do I feel so disconnected?

This is where it all began with me. I sat with tears flowing, trying to understand how I got to this place. I am this strong woman that so many depend on, but I was feeling as if I couldn't depend on me. I felt as if God couldn't depend on me and that's what was tearing me apart.

If this is where you are, then this very moment is where you need to be. On the pages of this journal you will gain the tools needed to answer these questions and then rebuild your relationship with God needed to birth your purpose.

Our spiritual health and physical well-being are intimately connected. We must begin the process of healing our physical man while moving towards making the spirit man whole again. To do this, we must look at the three major elements that comprise our being the mind, body, soul and then we must examine the physical and spiritual aspects.

All change starts with acceptance. What must I accept?

> I am not invincible.
> I can't do it all.
> There is only one me.

Week One

How quiet are you willing to be, to hear God?

I'll Rest When I'm Dead

We must believe God wants the best for us. This belief is based on the world around us. His desire is that our every need be met.

Why is rest an important element of your life's journey? The lack of rest is often the reason we become distracted. When you fail to get adequate rest, your spiritual man becomes disconnected from your physical man. The body was created to enter a state of rest. When the body is able to rest, your spirit-man is able to commune with the Holy Spirit. It is during this time that the purpose and power of God is infused in your being. This is when you have those dreams that are life-changing.

When you awake after adequate rest, you rise focused with a more determined mindset. If you try to go throughout your day repeatedly deprived of rest you're becoming a walking storm. Each day the winds and rains become increasingly stronger until the storm has completely wreaked havoc in every area of your life, pulling you farther and farther from God and all the things related to Him and His purpose for your life.

Day 1
I Need Rest

Statement of the Day: Rest is a vital element for our physical and spiritual man. It is during the time of rest that we are restored, repaired and refueled.

> Physically- When we fail to get adequate rest, it becomes hard to maintain mental sharpness. Our bodies are able to repair damages from the day.

> Spiritually- It is during times of rest that God can release ideas, transform mindsets and give insight. Our spirit can commune with God and get the refreshing rest that opens us up to genuine peace and consuming joy.

Scripture of the Day: Matthew 11:29

> *"Take my yoke upon you and learn from me, for I am gentle and humble in heart, and you will find rest for your souls."*

Your Goals for Today Are:

1. Stop and draw near to God. This is accomplished by first creating a welcoming atmosphere for Him. Try a few deep breaths and allow your mind to slowly release the stresses of the day. Then quote the Scripture of the day slowly. Lastly, ask God to meet you at this point of need.

2. Move to a place where you are allowing the adequate time for God to meet you in stillness. Seek God for His unwavering Spirit. It's in that place where you can release your cares, which allows your mind and heart to rest.

_____

_____

_____

_____

_____

_____

_____

_____

Day 2
Seek Peace

Statement of the Day: There is nothing more amazing than experiencing God's peace, love, joy and grace. It's the place that we should long to be.

> Physically- Peace is a place that our bodies long for. Peace is necessary for adequate rest. Peace allows your mind to be open to change.

> Spiritually- When you rest in the presence of God, your Spirit man is in a position to receive the fullness of God's Spirit, which allows you to obtain that, "peace that surpasses all understanding."

Scripture of the Day: Psalm 29:11

> *"The Lord gives strength to his people; the Lord blesses his people with peace."*

Your Goals for Today Are:

1. Draw near to God, by increasing your time of stillness with Him. Asking God to fill you once again with His Holy Spirit and to renew your mind.
2. Seek peace with a spirit of intention. By this you will have to be vocal, persistent, and specific.

>Say it, I will have peace today. Peace lives inside of me.
>Write it, I will have peace today. Peace lives inside of me.
>Think it, I will have peace today. Peace lives inside of me.

Day 3
Recalculate Me

Statement of the Day: There is nothing more calming than tapping into God when you have reached the point of feeling as if you are consistently scattered to and from. Running a maze franticly with no end in sight. Having a visual reminder of God's grace can pull you back into His presence.

Physically- When you tap into the peace of God, He is able to offer you His discerning spirit. The power of His spirit allows you to make a decision that is edifying to your physical well-being. You are conscience of what you allow into your body, how you treat your body and what your body produces.

Spiritually- It is through the spirit of Christ that we are recalculated. When we begin to move off course, God's Spirit will guide us back to the place where His presence soothes our worries, releases our stresses and strengthens our soul.

Scripture of the Day: Psalm 131:2

"But I have calmed and quieted myself, I am like a weaned child with its mother; like a weaned child I am content."

Your Goals Today Are:

1. Create a visual reminder of God's grace. Physically you can look at something as simple as your car's GPS or a navigational app on your phone and know if you were to move off course, God's grace will recalculate your location and help you move back into position

2. Mentally you can picture Jesus on the cross. Knowing that His death affords you the grace you so preciously receive each day.

_____

_____

_____

_____

_____

_____

_____

_____

_____

_____

Day 4
My Taste Buds Crave You

Statement of the Day: When you begin to form a relationship with God, all your senses will be affected. Your desire for His presence will become a craving for more time with Him.

Physically- Just as your physical body craves things such as chocolate, coffee, attention, and affection, so does your spirit. The endorphins that are released when that piece of chocolate hits your tongue and your entire body sighs, can also happen when you enter into God's presence.

Spiritually- When you spend time with God and His spirit lulls you to a place of spiritual rest, you will long to be in that place. Your physical and spiritual body will crave the attention God gives.

Scripture of the Day: Psalm 63:1

"You, God, are my God, earnestly I seek you; I thirst for you, my whole being longs for you, in a dry and parched land where there is no water."

Your Goals for Today Are:

1. Ask God to increase your heart's desire for Him.

2. Throughout the day affirm your love for Christ.
   God I love You
   God I desire Your will
   My heart desires Your love

_____

_____

_____

_____

_____

_____

_____

_____

_____

Day 5
Unclog My Mind

Statement of the Day: It is easy for your mind to become cluttered with the stresses of life. However, we must move to a place where we aim to declutter our minds in order to see and hear clearly from God.

Physically- When your mind is cluttered with the noise of the world, your body will begin to manifest outwardly the turmoil of the mental. The constant thoughts of home, work, kids, and finances will interrupt your sleep. You will find it hard to focus. You will create reminders for the reminders only to find yourself physically, emotionally and mentally drained. As you seek God to unclog your mind you will find that the process will be a constant struggle to reconnect your thoughts with His. You must limit what you allow to invade your mental.

Spiritually- The idle mind is often called, "The devil's playground." I challenge you to ring the bell and call recess to an end. Your mind is the place where ideas are planted, plans are designed and peace is stirred. You must draw near to God and occupy every piece of equipment on your playground to be filled with those things that are from Christ.

Scripture of the Day: Proverbs 23:33
"Your eyes will see strange sights, and your mind will imagine confusing things."

Your Goals for Today Are:

1. To ring the bell. The ringing of a bell is often a symbolic reminder that time is up. So today ring the bell. Physically find a bell, whether it's an app on an electronic device, you yourself whistling or the alarm clock.

2. Throughout the day when you begin to feel overwhelmed, stressed or drained, ring your proverbial bell.

_____

_____

_____

_____

_____

_____

_____

_____

Day 6
Quiet the Storms

Statement of the Day: Each day grants you new mercies from God. Along with His new mercies comes storms that aim to throw us overboard. You must tap into the power that God has left you to speak to the storm. Learn to be vocal. Let the storm know you are walking with the authority of the Almighty God.

Physically- There comes a point where you must recognize the power of God in your life. God has given you the power of the Holy Spirit. You can stand in confidence knowing that you can walk into each day armed with authority to quiet the storms of your life.

Spiritually- Some of the greatest storms in your life will be those you fight internally. Knowing what is right and doing what is right often causes much turmoil and grief. The spiritual storms will require private time, in silence, in the presence of God. Allow Him to whisper to your spirit how to defeat the wars that rage within.

Scripture of the Day: Luke 8:24

"The disciples went and woke him, saying, "Master, Master, we're going to drown!" He got up and rebuked the wind and the raging waters; the storm subsided, and all was calm."

Your Goals for Today Are:

1. Think about the storms of your life. Just as Jesus spoke to the storm and it calmed. We have the power to speak to those storms of our life. What are some things you can say to your storms?

2. Vocalize your truths.
> I have victory
> I will live and not die
> I walk in favor
> I am Blessed
> I have a window of Blessings assigned by God

_____

_____

_____

_____

_____

_____

_____

_____

Day 7
My Desire for Freedom

Statement of the Day: There will reach a point on this journey where your heart's desire will begin to grow and increase in intensity. It is now that you realize that there is no one greater than God. He is and will always be your constant resource, supplying your every want, need and desire.

Physically- Your prayer is not just to walk in the physical freedom of the land, but to experience the true freedom of the spiritual, emotional and mental that is found in Christ.

Spiritually- Seek God's help to break the ties of spiritual connections that doesn't bring glory to you or fulfill the desire and purpose that has been ordained for your life. Continually seek discernment, asking specifically for spiritual growth and sight.

Scripture of the Day: Ephesians 3:12

"In him and through faith in him we may approach God with freedom and confidence."

Your Goals for Today Are:

1. As you go throughout the day notice the many freedoms we take for grant.

2. Define what freedom means to you.

_____

_____

_____

_____

_____

_____

_____

_____

_____

Week Two

Are you willing to love yourself past the pain in order to connect with the purpose?

Self-Love

"Self-love is a state of appreciation for oneself that grows from actions that support our physical, psychological and spiritual growth. Self-love is dynamic; it grows by actions that mature us. When we act in ways that expand self-love in us, we begin to accept much better our weaknesses as well as our strengths, have less need to explain away our shortcomings, have compassion for ourselves as human beings struggling to find personal meaning, are more centered in our life purpose and values, and expect living fulfillment through our own efforts. " ~ Deborah Khoshaba Psy.D.~ psychologytoday.com

When you love who you are, it becomes easier to make decisions as it concerns your spiritual health and well-being. God wants you to love yourself, as He loves you. He wants you to grow yourself practicing the concepts in His word. ~Add to You~

As that love deepens your confidence in Christ is strengthened. You will begin to reevaluate which will lead to a deliberate transformation of your mindset towards self.

You become fully aware of your worth. Understanding that:
You are Rare (one of a kind)
You are Valuable (more than a precious jewel)
You are Authentic (you are an original, uniquely designed by God)
You are Love (being rooted and grounded in love, Ephesians 3:17)

The point where you become fully aware of who you are through Christ. It won't matter who comes or goes, what's done or said, because you will know who you are and whose you are.

Now that you are at a place where you understand the distractions and ready to become re-engaged, it is time to begin active labor. We need to look at some simple truths,

Become okay with being perfectly imperfect- You will make mistakes and it's okay. The goal is to learn from the mistake and then grow from the lesson learned.

Begin to track your progress - It is often easy to forget how far we've come, especially in times of trials. We are often so overwhelmed with the attacks that we fail to remember where we come from.

Gain Knowledge- You must spend time saturating your mind to gain understanding. Spend time in God's Word, read books, watch videos/livestreams or listen to messages that help you to understand you.

Day 8
Self-Love

Statement of the Day: Self-love is often a misunderstood concept. Being able to have an intimate relationship with Christ is where you will find the answers to the secret of authentic self-love. You most likely have given yourself relentlessly to others and often fall short of providing the nurturing needed for self.

Physically- Being able to love yourself will require you to love the skin you are in. Loving your imperfections, accepting your idiosyncrasies, being understanding that this will be a process will be the first steps in fostering a foundation for self-love.

Spiritually- Understanding that you were first rooted, by God in love, leads you to comprehend the depth of love. Self-love is more than surface level. It burrows deep to your spirit man. It is there that you connect with God. Once that connection is made, you will become grounded. Here is where you find that place of balance. With the guiding of the Holy Spirit you will begin to manifest outwardly that love for self that God has planted inwardly.

Scripture of the Day: Ephesians 3:17

"That Christ may dwell in your hearts through faith; that you, being rooted and grounded in love."

Your Goals for Today Are:

1. Mentally do an inventory of those physical attributes that you love about yourself.

2. As you proceed throughout the day notice the grass, flowers and trees. Think about how they are rooted in the earth. Notice the uniqueness and ponder, when have you seen a tree compare itself to the flower. So, why would you?

_____

_____

_____

_____

_____

_____

_____

_____

_____

_____

Day 9
Created in His Image

Statement of the Day: God's Word tells us how we are created in the image of the most High. In Genesis 1:27 you are told, **"So God created man in His own image."** Why would we want to change what God created? We will look at ourselves in the mirror and begin a critical analyzation of self, i.e., I wish I was taller/shorter, thinner/heavier, darker/lighter, and smarter. But, if everything created by God is good, then YOU are good! You are exactly who He intended you to be.

Physically- We were created in God's image! When was the last time you heard someone say, I'm really not feeling the way God looks right now? You know God needs to lose some weight? God needs a haircut? Okay why then are you scrutinizing yourself? Know that you are a uniquely designed masterpiece, created by a designer with exquisite taste.

Spiritually- Your physical body houses the true representation of God. Your Spirit. God is a spirit. It is in your spirit that you will connect with Him. Self-love is conceived in that special place where your spirit communes with God. When the spiritual transformation takes place, it will be evident in your outward appearance. There is something magnificent about the glow that radiates from your spirit. God's Spirit will teach you how to appreciate the vessel that is YOU, your body and spirit, He's entrusted to you.

Scripture of the Day: Genesis 1:27

"So God created mankind in his own image, in the image of God he created them; male and female he created them."

Your Goals for Today Are:

1. Take a long look at yourself in the mirror. Think about what God would have been thinking as He created you. How He loved you so much that He took the time to create you and not just speak you into existence. He made you with love.

2. Throughout the day whisper to yourself, God made me special with love.

_____

_____

_____

_____

_____

_____

_____

_____

_____

Day 10
Transform Me

Statement of the Day: Transformation is more than a physical change. True transformation requires a mental breaking. Much like the water breaking of a woman giving birth, a mental breaking signals the point of no turning back. You are ready to push through the distractions, connect with God and allow Him to transform you.

Physically- His word says you are fearfully and wonderfully made. God doesn't lie and His word doesn't return void. So, WALK in your wonderfulness! The new you requires a level of Holy Boldness. You are proud of the vessel God gifted you for His purpose.

Spiritually- Just as your physical body is able to experience a transformation, so is your Spirit. Spending time in God's presence and saturating your spirit with His word will bring about that spiritual transformation that matches your physical transformation.

Scripture of the Day: Ephesians 4:23-24

"and be renewed in the spirit of your mind, 24 and that you put on the new man which was created according to God, in true righteousness and holiness."

Your Goals for Today Are:

1. Affirm yourself by doing the following.
> Say it, I am Physically and Wonderfully made.
> Write it, I am Physically and Wonderfully made.
> Think it, I am Physically and Wonderfully made.

2. Thank God throughout the day for your transformation. Thank God for your new mindset, your "I Am" mindset.

_____

_____

_____

_____

_____

_____

_____

_____

_____

_____

Day 11
Let Me See Me

Statement of the Day: Often we hear beauty is in the eye of the beholder, yet we often fail to see the beauty that lies within ourselves. God looks at each of us lovingly through the eyes of the spirit. Knowing that He created us to do great works. We must seek to see ourselves as God sees us.

Physically- Being able to see the real you can sometimes be painful. We often proceed through life as if we have it all together. Hearing the comments of others as they proclaim how well you look, how well you carry yourself will lead to the false sense of, "I have it together." As we know, looks can be deceiving.

Spiritually- The same thing that happens physically, happens spiritually. We go to church on Sunday, we may even go to mid-week services, we give our tithes and/or offering and we think that God sees our efforts and knows our hearts, but what does the true condition of our heart looks like?

Scripture of the Day: Proverbs 30:12

"Those who are pure in their own eyes and yet are not cleansed of their filth."

Your Goals for Today Are:

1. Begin by asking God to let me see me. This will require you to do an inventory of your life. What does your life look like when the hat is removed, the masks are taken away, the people are gone? When it's just you and God, what do you see.

2. Create a list of at least two areas where you need God to show you His view of you.

_____

_____

_____

_____

_____

_____

_____

_____

_____

Day 12
A True Reflection

Statement of the Day: When you look in the mirror, does the reflection staring back at you represent a true mirror image of your heart?

Physically- Your physical body is a vessel gifted by God to you. Caring for your body is one way you can demonstrate a true reflection of Christ. However, when we allow the craziness of life to disrupt simple routines such as eating and resting, we risk distorting our Godly reflection.

Spiritually- As spiritual beings, we must understand the need for strong spiritual connections to Christ. We should see ourselves as the spiritual reflection of God, that's our true reflection,

Scripture of the Day: 1 Corinthians 6:19-20

"Do you not know that your bodies are temples of the Holy Spirit, who is in you, whom you have received from God? You are not your own; you were bought at a price. Therefore, honor God with your bodies."

Your Goals for Today Are:

1. Take a long look at yourself in the mirror. Don't just look at the physical features. Look in your eyes and ask yourself, does the person looking at me look to be happy, genuinely happy? Or, is this person exhibiting tiredness, sadness, sickness, and/or loneliness?

2. Now ask yourself, what is the source of the manifested image?

_____

_____

_____

_____

_____

_____

_____

_____

_____

_____

Day 13
One Me, Chosen by God

Statement of the Day: Being uniquely you, is what you must learn to love about yourself. Knowing that God has chosen you to think, love, be, and look different. Understand it's okay to be loud with a quiet spirit, to see the good in bad situations, to be strong and smart while remaining humble, laughing at the simplest of things, while crying at others. Different is okay. God chose you. There is only one you. Be you, embrace you, love you, and honor you because there will never be another you.

Physically- looking into the mirror it's often easy to pick out all the things you don't like about yourself. What would happen if you stopped picking apart the bad and started to appreciate the uniqueness of you. Look at that person in the mirror, with the understanding that there is no other person like you, on this Earth. You were created by God to be an original work of art.

Spiritually- there is something unique about each of us spiritually. Just as your DNA is unique to you it has some shared markers from your parents from whom you were conceived. That's why you have some similarities to your siblings or family members. So is it spiritually. We have DNA markers of our Father in Heaven. It is those shared markers that allows us to create spiritual connections. However, we are still unique spiritual individuals. With a purpose that is uniquely designed by God for only you.

Scripture of the Day: Ephesians 2:10

"For we are God's handiwork, created in Christ Jesus to do good works, which God prepared in advance for us to do."

Your Goals for Today Are:

1. Take a long look at yourself in the mirror and look at the physical features. Notice how each aspect of your face is intricately created. Consider the attention to detail that God gave. God did that! He took the time to fashion every inch of your body.

2. As you go through the day and catch a glimpse of yourself in passing, the rear-view mirror, the sliding doors, or a tinted window, thank God for the beauty that is you.

_____

_____

_____

_____

_____

_____

_____

_____

Day 14
A New Creation

Statement of the Day:

One person's trash is another person's treasure. The process of patchwork quilting takes various pieces of scrap material that are then sewn together in order to create something new. God can do the same thing to you. He can take the broken pieces of your life and fashion them into a new creation.

Physically- looking into the mirror at your reflection you can see pieces of your parents, ancestors and environment. Whether you have your father's nose, your momma's eyes, granny's smile or your brazen demeanor, all of these pieces be it genetics or attainment are what made you the person you see in the mirror.

Spiritually- there is something magical that happens when God uses your broken heart, broken spirit, and broken mind and begins to mold those pieces. God takes your broken pieces like clay and places them on His potter's wheel. With each spin, He infuses His love, grace, peace, and strength into the clay until you become His masterpiece, a new creation, ready to embrace their purpose.

Scripture of the Day: 2 Corinthians 5:17

"Therefore, if anyone is in Christ, he is a new creation; old things have passed away; behold, all things have become new."

Your Goals for Today Are:

1. Create a list of your broken pieces.

2. As you go throughout this day, take time to notice how many items have been recycled to create a new item.

_____

_____

_____

_____

_____

_____

_____

_____

_____

_____

_____

Week Three

When you release the guilt, you receive the gift.

Guiltless Selfishness

The word selfish is often used to describe those persons whose only focused on themselves even at the cost of others. Well on today, we will take back the negative power of the word and spin it for our betterment. You can learn to be selfish without the guilt. It's easy to start each day with a list of people to care for, deadlines to be met, chores to be completed, problems to be solved and just as quickly as the day starts, it's over. Now you sit wondering, "What did I accomplish today?" Playing the highlights of the day, processing what was done, what's left to do and what's to be added to tomorrow's list.

Merriam-Webster defines selfish as, *"concerned excessively or exclusively with oneself: seeking or concentrating on one's own advantage, pleasure, or well-being without regard for others."* What would happen if we took a positive spin and instead of, "without regard for others," you seek to focus on yourself with the expectation of being better for your tribe. You can't continue to fail to eat properly, rest properly or most importantly connect with God properly. You are doing a grave in service to those depending on you. Being selfish with you is important. Placing yourself first will allow you to better serve your family, friends, your employer/employees and most of all, it will allow you to flow in your purpose. When you neglect to spend the time needed to prepare you for the day, you miss out on the opportunity to receive the blessings and help that awaits you in God's presence.

Day 15
Today I Choose Me

Statement of the Day:

You have been conditioned to believe that placing yourself first is a bad thing. You are told it's better to give than receive. Today challenge yourself to transform your thinking. Your first question, if I am empty what can I give?

Physically-When you continually give your time and resources to others, it is easy to lose sight of your needs and become disconnected from who you are. Slowly your body begins to give you signs of your neglect. Constant fatigue and forgetfulness are the first telltale signs.

Spiritually-What develops physically is often a manifestation of your spiritual neglect. Your prayer or devotion times or journaling are usually the first things we abandon in order to free up time that is filled with doing for others. However, these entities are what you need so that you can receive from God in order to better give to others.

Scripture of the Day: Acts 3:19

"...so that times of refreshing may come from the presence of the Lord,"

Your Goals for Today Are:

1. Take Back Your "Selfishness"
Say it: It is okay to put me first.
Write it: I will schedule me time for myself on my calendar.
Think it: I am meant to be whole. It's okay to be selfish.

2. Own it! Take a 10-minute break and do nothing. During this time ask God to help you release the guilt associated with choosing you.

_____

_____

_____

_____

_____

_____

_____

_____

_____

Day 16
Time Out

Statement of the Day:

Are you in need of a time out? Time out is most often used as a form of discipline for young kids. The goal of a time out is to allow the child time to think about their unfavorable actions and their consequence. As adults, a timeout can be used to remove you from an unfavorable environment in order to reconnect with God and get His perspective on your life, choices and actions.

Physically- A time out will allow you to clear your head, reset your way of thinking and breathe deeply. All of these things will help you to hear from God more clearly. If the mind is the devil's playground, then it is time for you to ring the bell and call recess to an end. Today is the day you place satan in time out and reclaim your mind. God is speaking.

Spiritually- Jesus even understood the need for time out. When He was experiencing His most trying times, He would steal away to commune with God. He knew the importance of having an uncluttered mind in the midst of the chaos going on around Him.

Scripture of the Day: Matthew 26:36

36 Then Jesus came with them to a place called Gethsemane, and said to the disciples, "Sit here while I go and pray over there."

Your Goals for Today Are:

1. Put yourself in timeout. Schedule at least 30 minutes of alone time for you this week.

2. During your alone time, jot down the struggles keeping you from doing this more often.

_____

_____

_____

_____

_____

_____

_____

_____

_____

_____

_____

Day 17
Me First

Statement of the Day:

The thought of putting yourself first is most likely frightening. What will people think? What if something happens? Am I being selfish? The answer, no. You can't worry so much about the what if, that you neglect the but if. But if you'd trusted God to provide, but if you'd taken time to plan, but if you'd stop to rest. The what ifs lead to a lot of but ifs, which are usually in hindsight. Let's stop looking back and embrace the attitude of, me first."

Physically- In a medical emergency it's the job of the first responders to show up, assess the needs and render service. Now the first responder doesn't take the place of the doctor, but they stabilize the patient until they arrive to the hospital where the doctor awaits. You are the first responder of your life. You must show up first for you. Assess the damage. Render services: devotion, prayer, fasting and/or praise and watch the Doctor show up.

Spiritually- You are created in the image of God. Your body is to be presented as a living sacrifice to God because it is just that precious to Him. God understands how valuable you are. He knows that your physical body is the vessel He will use to bring about glory in the earth. Whether it's your hands, your mind, your voice, or your feet they are entrusted to you to care for. If God cannot trust you to care for the one body He gifted you, how can He trust you to care for the nations.

Scripture of the Day: Romans 12:1

[1] I beseech you therefore, brethren, by the mercies of God, that you present your bodies a living sacrifice, holy, acceptable to God, which is your reasonable service.

46

Your Goals for Today Are:

1. What ifs cause you to stop doing what you know is right. 2. What are some, "what if" statements you make?

2. Take back your power by placing yourself first. Start by creating your, "but if statements. But ifs are when you count up the cost.

_____

_____

_____

_____

_____

_____

_____

_____

_____

_____

Day 18
I am The Star

Statement of the Day:

There are millions of stars that light up the sky. On a clear night, you can see the sky and all of its majesty. However, on a cloudy or overcast night sky you may not be able to see a single star. You want to know a secret? Just because you don't see it's shine doesn't mean it's any less of a star. The same goes for you. Just because you have been distracted and the weight of the world has you discouraged does not make you any less of a star in the eyes of God. Don't allow past failures, mistakes or trials to guilt you into dimming your shine. You are a star.

Physically- It is easy to look at the next person and think how they have it all together. They are running a business, a household and look fabulous every day. Then in your mind, begin to self-evaluate. Comparing yourself to others is like looking at the stars through a broken telescope. The view is distorted.

Spiritually- God cares so much about you, that He took the time to breathe the very breath of life into your lungs. He did not merely speak you into existence, but created you with labor and time. He wants you to understand that same importance as it speaks to self-care. You can't be guilty when you invest labor and time into your purpose.

Scripture of the Day: 1 Corinthians 15:40-41

[40] "There are also celestial bodies and terrestrial bodies; but the glory of the celestial is one, and the glory of the terrestrial is another. [41] There is one glory of the sun, another glory of the moon, and another glory of the stars; for one star differs from another star in glory."

Your Goals for Today Are:

1. As the sun sets on this evening, take a moment to gaze out at the sky. Consider how much more God loves you if He made you as unique as the stars.

2. Great a list of your unique characteristics and mannerisms.

_____

_____

_____

_____

_____

_____

_____

_____

_____

_____

_____

Day 19
Today I Say No

Statement of the Day:

Do you struggle with being able to say no? Is your failure to say no part of the reason you are distracted and disconnected? The times you do get the courage to say no are you left with an overwhelming feeling of guilt? Guess what. You are not alone. You are not the first person to be here. It is time to take back the power of your no. Yes, no has power. No releases guilt. No reduces stress. No can evoke restful sleep. No can restore peace.

Physically-The body doesn't categorize bad stress from good stress. However, the body can differentiate pain from pleasure. Guilt and stress are painful to the body while restful sleep and peace brings pleasure. So, do yourself a favor and reclaim life's pleasures.

Spiritually- God wants you to stand boldly, armed with the power that comes with no. God has promised you an abundant life with the security of knowing He desires only the best for you. He wants you to know how powerful you are.

Scripture of the Day: Isaiah 54:17

"No weapon formed against you shall prosper, And every tongue which rises against you in judgment You shall condemn. This is the heritage of the servants of the Lord, And their righteousness is from Me," Says the Lord."

Your Goals for Today Are:

1. Take a stroll down memory lane. List some of the yeses you should have said no to.

2. Build your no arsenal. List five ways you can say no.
       (save these, you'll need them soon).

_____

_____

_____

_____

_____

_____

_____

_____

_____

Day 20
Why Not Me?

Statement of the Day:

It is easy to ask God why me. When is the last time you have asked, why not me? Why should you not make time for yourself? Why should you not enjoy uninterrupted time with God? Why would you not enjoy a cup of coffee, warm croissant or piece of chocolate? When you experience moments like these something strange happens. Deep down you get an overwhelming feeling of guilt. Your mind then questions why are you sitting here, there's laundry to be done, kids to be fed, dishes to be washed, errands to be completed, and reports to be run. Then you become programmed to not place yourself first because that would be selfish, right? Wrong. Why not me? Why not me before the laundry? Why not me before the dishes? Why not me before the reports? Take back your, why me and trade it in for a, "why not me?

Physically- Being selfish with your time and resources is believed to be a bad thing. However what God has for you is for you. If you come to a four-way stop and you are the first car at the stop sign, then why would you wait for all the other cars to go. You were in position to be first to move, so move.

Spiritually- If God has ordered your steps and He is delighted in your ways then you owe it to Him to take the steps. Stop side tracking, stalling or flat out not moving and take those steps that have already been ordered. Only you can step for you. There is no guilt in walking in your purpose.

Scripture of the Day: Psalms 37: 23-24

23The steps of a good man are ordered by the Lord, And He delights in his way. 24 Though he fall, he shall not be utterly cast down; For the Lord upholds him with His hand.

Your Goals for Today Are:

1. Think about the steps you make today, remind yourself of God's delight with you. What are some ways God delights in you?

2. No one likes to fail; however failure brings levels of wisdom. What are some areas you are seeking wisdom for? List them.

_____

_____

_____

_____

_____

_____

_____

_____

_____

_____

Day 21
I Say So

Statement of the Day:

Your voice is one of the most powerful weapons you have. When you finish a statement with the words, "I say so," with an authoritative tone there is an expectation of finality. Overtime you have allowed others to quiet your voice. However, your voice needs to be heard and understood. There is nothing selfish about stating how you feel. Own your feelings. Own your voice.

Physically-In a quiet room or office space, a loud and boisterous voice will pierce the air and demand attention. That's where you are today. You are in a place that demands attention. You have to pay attention to you on today, I say so.

Spiritually- In the beginning, God spoke everything into existence. He began each statement with the authoritative words, "Let there be." There was no question as to what He expected. He spoke with the expectation that His words would be manifested. In the same spirit, you can speak with Godly boldness..

Scripture of the Day: Genesis 1:6-7

6Then God said, "Let there be a firmament in the midst of the waters, and let it divide the waters from the waters." 7 Thus God made the firmament, and divided the waters which were under the firmament from the waters which were above the firmament; and it was so.

Your Goals for Today Are:

1. Take back your voice today. What are some statements you need to make and end with, "I say so." Write at least two.

2. Recite these affirmations throughout the day.
    My voice has power.
    My voice is power.
    I am my voice.
    I am power
    I say so.

_____

_____

_____

_____

_____

_____

_____

_____

_____

Week 4

Reminders are visible when you're connected to the visionary.

Unleash the ReFactor

Out of brokenness you are often left feeling hurt and afraid. You've lost hope in man. You may cry out to God for peace. You may feel as if having a glass of wine will help soothe the pain. Or that with each roll of a blunt your problems will go up in smoke or maybe a loving touch will ignite the spark your spirit is in need of. For some, your drug of choice may be a triple chocolate, chocolate chunk cookie with chocolate drizzle to give you a momentary escape with each bite. While in the moment it feels, you've escaped the madness that is life. However, when it's all said and done, the bottle is empty, the smoke has cleared and the plate is empty, you are still broken.

As women, there is a tendency to over-compensate and when it seems as if we are losing control, we turn to quick fixes. But what if you were to allow your brokenness to birth your purpose. What if your brokenness was intended to release those people, detach from those things and abandon that which is killing your purpose? What if the pain was to serve as the pressure you need to press out those habits you can't break in and of yourself? What if God is pushing you in your brokenness to birth your Divine purpose. God wants to break through those strongholds whether they are physical, mental or spiritual.

Day 22
ReMember

Statement of the Day:

Your goal must be to break the silence and bring back to remembrance the purpose lying dormant inside of you. Your praise must be vocal. You must speak with the boldness and confidence that God has placed in you through His Holy Spirit.

Physically- There are occasions when a sound or smell will bring back to your remembrance a moment from your past. There is something special that happens when a fond childhood memory arises. It can take you back to that place mentally, physically, emotionally, and spiritually. Certain sounds, smells and images can do that. Of course, all memories from the past are not pleasant. There are those that you will want to push to the deep crevices of your memory banks to never relieve. What you have to remember is that your memory has a purpose. It is the key to you shunning or shining.

Spiritually- Your spirit is Divinely connected to God. The Holy Spirit allows us to remember the goodness of God. It allows the Word to bring back to your remembrance all that God has planned for you. Even those hard to remember memories, trials, failures and disappointments, God will allow you to see how He can and will use those to progress your towards your purpose.

Scripture of the Day: John 14:26

26 But the Helper, the Holy Spirit, whom the Father will send in My name, He will teach you all things, and bring to your remembrance all things that I said to you.

Your Goals for Today Are:

1. Take a stroll down memory lane. List a couple of tough life lessons you've had to learn.

2. Now list testimonies of God's presence in those situations.

_____

_____

_____

_____

_____

_____

_____

_____

_____

_____

Day 23
ReMind

Statement of the Day: Have you ever had to write a sticky note for your sticky note or set an alarm on your calendar to remind you of an appointment? What happens in your mind that causes you to need a reminder? Our minds become overwhelmed with the cares of the day.

Physically- Just as reminders are used to bring back to our remembrance those things we need to do, situations we need to resolve or people we need to call, you have symbols, scriptures, hymns and people that are reminders for you when you become distracted, disconnected and disengaged. The Cross, the Bible and most importantly the Holy Spirit.

Spiritually- You have to move to a place where you are continually asking the Holy Spirit to send you reminders. Reminder of God's promises, reminders of your victory, reminders of your gifts and reminders of your greatness.

Scripture of the Day: 2 Timothy 1:6-7

"Therefore I remind you to stir up the gift of God which is in you through the laying on of my hands. 7 For God has not given us a spirit of fear, but of power and of love and of a sound mind."

Your Goals for Today Are:

1. List at least two gifts you know that God has planted in you.

2. Find scriptures that will affirm these gifts and list them.

_____

_____

_____

_____

_____

_____

_____

_____

_____

_____

Day 24
ReDiscover

Statement of the Day:

The chaos of life will cause you to ignore or bury those things that you were once passionate about. Those visions before the kids or those dreams from childhood. You forgot the plans that were made, the dreams you dreamt and the visions God planted. The plans were placed on hold because you needed to put someone else's needs in front of yours, (a spouse, a child, a parent or other family member). The dreams have turned to fantasies because the plans are no longer there to ensure you stayed on track. The vision has faded because you have traveled away from the Source. But something magnificent happens when you begin to move back into position. As you move closer to the source, God will help you regain vision. Once the vision is restored you will rediscover those forgotten dreams. When you rediscover those dreams that have been buried, a small flame will begin to burn reigniting your passion. The passion flame will push you back to the source who will help you to plan, plant and harvest the purpose.

Physically-As a child we are filled with dreams of when I grow up. There is a desire to do whatever it takes to make those dreams come true, then life happens. Then you discover that the needs of others will take the place of yours and you will slowly, more and more, push your needs to the back. Whether it's a relationship, the birth of a baby, the death of a loved one, a failed class or business, something comes along and places your plans, dreams and visions on hold. Life will cause you to stop and rethink your plans.

Spiritually- God as stated in His word how you can find life in and through Him. Life has a way of stripping you of the promises of God. You may feel you have found a nice and predictable flow for your life, but what does it profit you to gain the world if you have forgotten the purpose. Reconnect and Rediscover.

Scripture of the Day: Matthew 16:25-26

"For whoever desires to save his life will lose it, but whoever loses his life for My sake will find it. [26] For what profit is it to a man if he gains the whole world, and loses his own soul? Or what will a man give in exchange for his soul?"

Your Goals for Today Are:

1. What have you forgotten? List a vision or dream that you once had plans of fulfilling, but has since become a fantasy.

2. Today pray continuously throughout the day for God to rekindle the flame of discovery. To help you rediscover that woman you forgot.

_____

_____

_____

_____

_____

_____

_____

_____

_____

Day 25
ReNew

Statement of the Day: A renewal signifies that there was something there and for whatever reason there was a disconnect of. Today is the day you ReNew your relationship with God. God has entered into a covenant relationship with you through the death and resurrection of His son Jesus. As for whatever your reason you have allowed this to become strained to the point of brokenness. God stands with open arms waiting for you to Renew that vow to Him and enter back into the covenant relationship.

Physically- Unlike your driver's license, car insurance or certifications there is no expiration date. Once you enter into covenant with God, you are given the right to spend eternity with Him. You don't have to worry about lapses or expirations specified by Him. God doesn't change or move from His position, but the awesomeness of God understands our free will spirit and if for any reason you lapse in your faith or allow your relationship with Him to expire, He waits unrequitedly for your vow of renewal.

Spiritually- There is a covenant relationship that God wants to form with You. It may seem as if you are too lost for this relationship, but God begs to differ. He wants you to recognize the distance that has come between you and Him, acknowledge and ReNew it.

Scripture of the Day: Exodus 9:16

But indeed for this purpose I have raised you up, that I may show My power in you, and that My name may be declared in all the earth.

Your Goals for Today Are:

1. List two areas in your life that you need to renew with God.

2. Write your renewal vow to God.

_____

_____

_____

_____

_____

_____

_____

_____

_____

Day 26
RePair

Statement of the Day:

You can't make it through this life without experiencing some form of brokenness. However you can't allow a season of brokenness to block you from walking in wholeness. God can fix what is broken if you allow Him to do the Repairs.

Physically- Whether you break a cellphone, nail or even a bone you understand that if a RePair is possible, it will take someone who is skilled and authorized in that area of brokenness to make that repair. You would not go to see an orthopedic surgeon for a broken iPhone just like you wouldn't go to your local nail tech to fix a broken leg. Then why would you go to your Creator to Repair your brokenness.

Spiritually- There is something that happens when you become broken. Your broken heart, mind and spirit are living sacrifices to Him. When you offer that sweet-smelling aroma to Him, He is able to take those broken pieces to birth your purpose.

Scripture of the Day: Psalm 51:16-17

[16]*For You do not desire sacrifice, or else I would give it; You do not delight in burnt offering.* [17]*The sacrifices of God are a broken spirit, A broken and a contrite heart— These, O God, You will not despise.*

Your Goals for Today Are:

1. Take a look at the areas in your life where you have experienced brokenness. Assess the damage and list at least three areas.

2. File the Claim. It is now time to go to Customer Service and Claim what's yours.

_____

_____

_____

_____

_____

_____

_____

_____

_____

_____

Day 27
ReClaim

Statement of the Day:

What God has promised you has not been repossessed by Him. You have allowed life to shift your vision, clutter your mind and deafen His voice. Today is the day that you ReClaim what is rightfully yours. Jesus paid for your purpose, in full, with His life. You won't need a black card to ReClaim the promises of God. You have a *Red Cross*. Seize what's yours.

Physically- If you are in a store and hear a voice over the intercom announce, "If you've lost a set of keys, please come to customer service to claim them." You understand that all the person needs to do is go up and claim what's theirs.

Spiritually- There was a price paid for you to walk in victory. When God sent His son to walk this earth, bear our sins and die for our redemption He paid that price. Everything that God has promised you is at the customer service desk. Step up and claim what's yours.

Scripture of the Day: Psalm 37:3-4

Trust in the Lord, and do good; Dwell in the land, and feed on His faithfulness. Delight yourself also in the Lord, And He shall give you the desires of your heart

Your Goals for Today Are:

1. Rejoice, knowing you have the power to Reclaim what is rightfully yours.

2. Reclaim what has been lost, stolen and destroyed:
    Let the Wallowing become Worship.
    Let the Pity become Praise.
    Let the Resentment lead to Redemption.
    Let the Bitterness open way to Blessings.

_____

_____

_____

_____

_____

_____

_____

_____

Day 28
ReConnect

Statement of the Day:

You must Break the Stereotypes- you are an overcomer who has been promised victory. It's time to ReConnect with your birth right by releasing that emotional and mental baggage and seizing the promises granted to you from the cross. In Acts 16 you read how Paul and Silas sat in a dark, dirty and damp prison shackled after being beaten. Instead of retreating they used what was in them to ReConnect with what they knew was ordained by God. In the same way you need to stir up your war cry and ReConnect with God.

Physically- A telephone line allows the communication process to happen between people who are not physically in the same location and are not able to see each other. If during a conversation, your call is dropped, redial the number to reconnect with the caller. You can do the same thing when you feel as if your conversation with God has been dropped. Jesus is still on the line you only need to call Him.

Spiritually- Prayer is your direct link to God. When you begin to pray, and call on the name of Jesus you grant your spirit man access to your Father in Heaven. Prayer and praise are the cables that will ReConnect you to your source, power and purpose.

Scripture of the Day: Acts 16:24-56

24 Having received such a charge, he put them into the inner prison and fastened their feet in the stocks. 25 But at midnight Paul and Silas were praying and singing hymns to God, and the prisoners were listening to them.

Your Goals for Today Are:

1. List at least three songs that serve as your spiritual war cry.

2. List at least two areas where you need to Reconnect to Christ.

_____

_____

_____

_____

_____

_____

_____

_____

_____

_____

Make the Connection

A penny on the ground is often overlooked, because of its value, based on society's standards. How valuable is that penny to a person who doesn't have anything? Are you a penny? Has society counted you out? Are you ready to make the connection?

You are now at a pivotal point in your life. Now that you understand that you've been introduced to the idea of guiltless selfishness, the necessity of rest, the responsibility of loving yourself and discovered your ReFactor, it is time to connect with the new you and the life God has destined for you to live. While your gifts will make room for you, the anointing will require you to make room for the forgotten you. The anointing will be the sealant that reconnects you with the vision, voice and the purpose God created for your life.

Something happens when reconciliation takes place. You come to an understanding that Christ is the only way and how He is the lover of your soul. Your strength is renewed. Your spirit is renewed and your joy restored as your desire to see His desire for your life manifests.

My Prayer

Father God, thank you for loving me, even when I could not love myself. Thank you for the purpose you've planted inside of me, even when I wasn't deserving. Thank you for the daily reminders. Help me to see and hear those reminders sent to keep me connected to you. Allow me to be a willing and yielding vessel, open to your discerning spirit. Allow my eyes to see, my ears to hear and my heart to feel Your reminders. Keep me on the path of purpose. My desire is to see you glorified in my life, to experience your desires for my life and to reconnect to the woman I forgot.

In Jesus name, I pray.
Amen

The Reminder

Each day we are given reminders that are sent to keep us on this journey, headed towards our destiny. Distractions come and cause us to miss those moments. God hasn't forgotten the vision, He didn't change His mind and the words He spoke to you shall not return void.

You completed the first steps towards reconnection. Today I want to remind God of His promises. Not because He's forgotten, but to remind Him that you know, that He knows, that you know, He can trust you with the vision. You see the reminder isn't for God, but for you. When you remind God of His promises towards you, you will strengthen your desire towards Him.

What do you want to REMIND God of today?

_____

_____

_____

_____

_____

_____

_____

_____

_____

ABOUT THE AUTHOR

Lyvonne Copeland, teacher, speaker and author is passionate about business and ministry. An Inspirational speaker with a passion for teaching, her style is very hands on and visual. She engages her audience with a candor that allows them to become fully engaged.

Lyvonne has a desire for helping women gain the understanding of their spiritual value and worth. She understands how the weight of life can cause women to become distracted and disconnected from the spiritual voice that pilots them towards their purpose. She aims to serve as the midwife for those women who are ready to birth that power that lies dormant inside of them by helping them identify the physical and spiritual intimacy that must be conjoined to the point of conception of their purpose.